CW00848373

Badminton Tips:
Bite-Size Techniques to
Boost Your Game

Ed Tennyson

Badminton Tips: Bite-Size Techniques To Boost Your Game

ISBN-13: 978-1466233843

ISBN-10: 1466233842

PART 1

How to Play Badminton - The Basics

Regardless of whether you're playing a game for fun or for competition, you still need to practice rigorously in order to win.

Furthermore, you need adequate preparation and the right attitude in order to emerge the winner.

This rule also holds true if you want to learn how to play badminton.

The good thing about playing badminton is that it can deliver a lot of benefits to your health, and that may be the reason why many people have taken to playing the game both as a leisure and a fitness activity.

Fitness enthusiasts consider badminton as an excellent way of toning up their muscles and burning excess fats.

So, badminton can actually improve your lifestyle as well.

However, if you're thinking about playing this game at a more competitive level, and if you actually want to make a career out of this sport, then you definitely need to practice it with a winning attitude.

To accomplish your goals, you have to be very serious about learning and practicing the game.

Playing the Game

The aim of badminton is to hit the shuttlecock over the net towards your opponent in such a way that he will not be able to return it.

This means you need to develop the skill of hitting the shuttlecock in different directions.

You can chose to hit hard or hit delicately, but your purpose should remain the same, which is to hit the shuttle towards your opponent's court such that he can't return it.

This may sound simple, but it actually requires constant practice and good training.

You may take training lessons from a professional badminton player or coach.

Online Lessons

Other than actual training from a coach or professional player, you also have the option of enrolling in an online badminton training program.

The main difference, of course, is that you'll be taking lessons within the comforts of your own home, in front of your computer screen rather than in a court.

This is an ideal solution for those who do not have the opportunity to join a physical badminton club and regularly go to the court for training sessions.

You can join a virtual badminton club instead and learn to play the game through videos.

As a newbie to this game, you can definitely learn a lot from online badminton training videos.

Furthermore, these videos will help you understand the techniques adopted by professional badminton players, especially as regards the forehand and backhand grips, among other things.

The good thing about virtual badminton clubs is that they offer several videos to teach you several different badminton techniques.

And you can use a video as many times as you need to master a particular technique.

Online badminton training programs and virtual clubs also provide you with some very important lessons, tips, and strategies to help you dominate the game.

Furthermore, they provide you with information on badminton equipment and accessories that you need when playing the game.

While your skill is the most important factor in becoming a good badminton player, the right equipment and accessories will help you achieve your goals as a player.

Simply by following the tips above, you can look forward to someday becoming a badminton player whom others can look up to.

So, take up your racket, enrol in a training program, and start practicing your badminton moves now!

PART 2
How to Be a Good
Badminton Player

In order to be a good badminton player, you need to have both physical skill and mental strength.

And to complement these two pre-requisites, you would also do well to learn about proper sports nutrition, especially if you're planning to play badminton competitively and are preparing for a tournament.

Read on to find out exactly how you can develop these three things and make sure that the next time you join a tournament, you'll be able to work your way up to the top.

Strokes

Basic badminton strokes include overhead forehand and backhand clear/drop/smash, lifts, drives, and net shots.

You can learn each of these strokes through a demo video.

Once you've learned how to execute each stroke correctly, you'll need to practice constantly and consistently until you're able to execute all strokes easily and effortlessly.

Footwork

Good footwork always works hand-in-hand with the ability to deliver strokes effectively.

A good badminton player necessarily has excellent coordination between his footwork and strokes.

This means his feet, arms, body, and swing should all be properly coordinated.

Stamina

Take note that a badminton match can last anywhere from 15 minutes to more than an hour and in a tournament, you may have to play more than one match in a day.

Furthermore, each badminton match follows a best-of-three-games rule, which means you'll have to play at least 2 successive games.

Therefore, you'll definitely need adequate stamina to perform successfully in any tournament.

Stamina can be built over time through regular strength training, cardio workouts, and other exercises.

And more than just building stamina, regular workouts will also help improve your game by increasing arm strength.

Strategy

You may already have the necessary skill and stamina, but without an excellent strategy, you're still likely to experience much difficulty in trying to win a badminton game.

You'll have to develop a strategy that allows you to make the right shot at the right time.

You should also be able to identify your opponent's weakness and exploit it.

It's especially crucial in a doubles game for you to identify the opposing pair's weakness and attack the weaker player.

You need to lay out a game plan before the match, but you should also be able to think quickly and make the right choice during the game itself.

Mental Strength

This is the most important element to ensure that you're able to make the right decisions even when you're under pressure during a badminton game.

For example, when you're nearing match point, you need the ability to stay focused regardless of whether you're leading or trailing.

Mental strength also allows you to change strategy in the middle of a game whenever the situation calls for it.

Remember that a good badminton player never goes down without a fight.

Sports Nutrition

Good nutrition is very important in maintaining your health and physical strength.

Proper nutrition involves consuming a well-balanced diet with just the right amount of carbohydrates, fats, protein, vitamins, minerals, electrolytes, and water.

You may want to consult a qualified nutritionist to help you prepare a good diet plan.

Remember that you need to drink water before, during, and after a match in order to maintain your health and to keep your body in top condition.

PART 3
Best Basic Badminton Skills You Should Learn

You probably know by now that the key to becoming a good badminton player lies in strengthening your skills in the very basics of the game.

In fact, the more familiar you are with the game's basics, the more easily you can improve your overall skills in the game.

Now, have you ever wondered why most of the top badminton players come from Asia and Europe?

Here's why:

In Asia and Europe, parents usually bring their kids to badminton courts during the weekend, and it's common for fathers to teach their children the basics of the game.

This means the kids are able to familiarize themselves with basic badminton techniques while they're young.

As they grow, these kids start to play the game with their group of friends.

By this time, they're already in a good position to explore further badminton skills and develop their prowess in more advanced techniques.

Badminton is more than just a game in many Asian and European countries; it's also a way for families and friends to maintain relationships.

The point is that you really need to learn the basic badminton skills at the outset.

Once you've mastered the basics, you don't even have to learn the advanced techniques because you'll be able to naturally develop them!

Executing top-quality deceptions, delivering strong smashes, and defending against a smash will come more easily to you.

And badminton will become even more exciting for you once you develop these skills.

So, the importance of learning badminton basics can't be emphasized enough for those who want to become a good badminton player.

Among the most important basic skills you need to master in the sport of badminton are gripping technique and the full arm swing, which is also known as the basic badminton stroke.

Gripping technique refers to the right way of gripping a badminton racket, which allows you to transfer more power into your strokes.

Once you've mastered this and the basic badminton swing, then you'll be better able to perform a clear, a drop shot, or even a deadly badminton smash.

Another basic badminton technique you need to familiarize yourself with is the footwork.

Remember that badminton is essentially a game of speed, which necessitates effective and organized footwork, allowing you to move quickly around the court during a game.

Becoming a good badminton player is really as simple as learning, practising, and mastering these three basic skills, but it does take a lot of hard work.

After you've learned and mastered the basics, you may begin exploring more advanced skills and techniques in badminton.

These include the following:

1. Fast attacks involving maximum wrist action;

2. Attacking clear;

3. Net kill; and

4. Deception

So, there you have it: in order to dominate a game of badminton, you'll first have to learn the basics, master them through constant practice, and then move on to more advanced techniques.

Soon, you should be well on your way towards a much better performance in a badminton game.

And who knows, in time you may even be able to hold your own in a game against even the top Asian and European players!

PART 4

Fundamental Badminton Techniques

If you want to become a better badminton player, then you should practice the basic techniques of the game consistently.

Even if you play only for recreation, it's still a good idea to strive to improve your badminton skills.

Here are the six basic badminton techniques you need to master:

1. The grip

Having the right grip is the foundation for being a good badminton player.

To get more power and accuracy into your strokes, make sure you're holding your racket correctly.

The two main types of grips are the forehand and the backhand grip.

The forehand grip is used when taking shots in front of your body, holding the handle of your racket as if you were shaking hands.

The backhand grip is used when taking shots from behind, turning the racket counter-clockwise.

2. Footwork

Remember that your opponent will try his best to keep the shuttle away from you, so you should be prepared to move very quickly and accurately around the court, and this can be done easily with good footwork.

You'll need to know how to skip, shuffle, glide, lunge, and bounce to your advantage.

You should keep your knees slightly bent and you should be ready to move at all times.

3. Serving

Knowing how to serve right can be an excellent way of earning easy points.

The basic kinds of badminton serve are low serve, high serve, drive serve, and flick serve.

You'll be better able to choose which serve to use after observing your opponent.

For example, if your opponent likes to stay close to the net, then it's best to deliver a high serve to the back of the court.

4. The Smash

This is a powerful move every aspiring badminton player should master.

It's a downward shot coming steeply down into your opponent's forecourt or midcourt area.

To add power to your smash, you can opt to jump and then make the shot as you come down.

This will give your opponent very little time to react, thus almost guaranteeing that you win the point.

Be careful not to overuse the smash, though, as that might tire you out.

5. The Drive

If the shuttle falls too low for you to hit a smash, you can choose to execute a drive instead.

This type of shot has the shuttle moving horizontally instead of arching upward.

The shuttle just skims the top of the net either in a diagonal direction or straight from your shooting position.

The goal is for you to get the shuttle behind your opponent such that he'll have a difficult time returning the shot.

6. Net Play

This shot is usually executed just by moving your wrist, and it lacks the power of the other techniques.

The goal in using this shot is to gently knock the shuttle over the net such that your opponent cannot reach it in time.

Such a light shot very near the net is difficult to return, especially if you can somehow get the shuttle tumbling.

It is best used when your opponent is too far from the net to react in time.

PART 5
Important Badminton Strokes Every Beginner Should Learn

If you're a beginner in the game of badminton, then you're likely to wonder what particular skills or techniques you need to master in order for you to become a good player.

Of course, there are a lot of badminton skills and techniques you should learn, but there are some basic strokes you need to master first before moving on to more complex aspects of the game such as net plays and smashes.

Here are the six basic badminton strokes you need to learn by heart:

1. Forehand Stroke

This is a simple forehand swing motion, but it's the basic stroke you need to master in order for you to learn all of the other badminton strokes.

Once you're able to hit a good forehand stroke, it'll be much easier to learn how to do a badminton clear, drop, and even a smash.

2. Forehand Clear

This is the foremost defensive shot in the sport of badminton.

It's a shot where you hit the shuttle high into the air, with the goal of landing it at the farthest baseline of your opponent's area of the court.

If you're able to execute this shot successfully, your opponent will have a hard time returning the shot, and even if he is able to return it, he won't be able to do much to attack.

3. Forehand Drop

Aside from a good defensive shot, you can also benefit from learning an effective semi-defensive/offensive shot in order to win badminton rallies.

The forehand drop is one such shot.

It is done from the back of your court, hitting the shuttle such that it gets into the front area of your opponent's side of the court.

A perfectly executed drop shot can be very effective in winning you a point.

At the same time, it's also considered a good defensive shot because a good drop shot eliminates all options for your opponent to execute an offensive shot.

4. Backhand Stroke

If you opponent hits the shuttle towards your backhand area, then you should position yourself such that you can return the shot with a forehand stroke.

Alternatively, you can execute a good backhand stroke to prevent your opponent from winning the point.

This stroke is a simple swing using the backhand grip.

5. Backhand Drop

Many badminton players are unable to execute good backhand strokes.

A possible reason for this is that many people find it difficult to switch quickly from a forehand to a backhand grip.

There are even people who really can't execute a good backhand stroke even when they're already using a backhand grip.

You can work on your backhand skill by practicing the backhand drop.

This shot doesn't require much strength because the aim is just to get the shuttle over the net, just like in a forehand drop.

6. Backhand Clear

This is one shot many badminton players find difficult to execute.

That's probably the reason why smart players always attack their opponent's backhand area.

So, if you want to be a really good badminton player, you'll have to work on your backhand skills.

A weak backhand stroke doesn't mean you're weak; most of the time, it only means you lack the correct backhand grip technique and swing motion.

When executing a backhand clear, try getting the shuttle to travel as high as possible.

PART 6
How to Improve Your Performance

So, you've learned and mastered all the basic badminton skills and techniques. Is that enough to give you a win?

Well, it'll certainly help a lot, but it's not quite enough.

There are a few other factors that can affect your performance as a badminton player, and you'll have to take these factors into consideration if you truly want to be good at the sport.

Here's how you can avoid a bad performance during a badminton game:

1. Get adequate rest

Adequate rest is essential in making you deliver optimum performance during a game.

It's almost impossible to concentrate on the game when you're tired and sleepy, right?

40

Quick reflexes and intense focus are very important in badminton, so you'll really need to be well-rested before engaging in a game.

Make sure you have at least eight hours of sleep every night so you'll be able to give your best anytime you're on the court.

2. Stay hydrated

Water is vital to the normal functions of your body, and being dehydrated can make you lethargic, mess up your concentration, and may even cause a mild headache, which will make it even more difficult for you to focus on your game.

Be sure to drink at least eight glasses of water each day, and even more during workouts.

3. Eat before a game

Remember that a badminton game requires lots of energy, which means you probably won't be able to play at peak levels when you're hungry.

That's because food is your main source of energy.

With enough energy, you'll be able to move faster, strike harder, and strategize better.

Make sure, though, that you take your meal about an hour and a half to allow enough time for digestion.

If, anytime during the game, you feel an energy slump, you may simply consume an energy bar or some sports drink to get powered up again.

4. Quit bad habits

If you're serious about improving your game in badminton, then you most definitely should stop bad habits such as smoking and drinking.

Smoking is harmful to your health in general, and in terms of sports, it can dramatically affect your level of fitness.

Smokers are likely to have much less stamina as compared to non-smokers.

Drinking, on the other hand, can slow down your reflexes.

5. Warm-up and Stretching

It's very important to warm-up before engaging in any strenuous physical activity.

This loosens your muscles and helps prevent injury during the activity.

After the warm-up, you should also do some stretching for 15-20 minutes.

This is true whether you're training or getting ready for an actual game.

Stretching not only reduces the risk for injury, but also enables you to move faster and reach out further during the game.

6. Get the right equipment

Don't get ripped off by immediately going for the most expensive badminton equipment.

Remember that high price doesn't necessarily mean top quality.

Before you even consider the price, make sure you choose the right equipment based on quality first.

Take your shoes, for example, badminton requires very quick footwork, so you'll definitely have to make sure you have the right shoes for it.

Otherwise, you'll be in danger of having ankle or knee injuries.

Choosing the right badminton racket is also very important, as it can increase your performance level.

What's important is for you to choose a racket that suits your style of play and enhances your strength as a player.

PART 7
Exercises to Improve Your Footwork

You're aware that good footwork is essential in badminton, and you're probably looking for ways of improving your own footwork so you can become a much better badminton player.

Remember that there are two aspects to badminton footwork – travelling to the shuttle and recovery.

Unfortunately, many players often take recovery for granted.

So, the next time you do shuttle runs, shadow badminton, pattern drills, or fast feet exercises, try to pay more attention to your recovery footwork.

You'll be amazed at the improvement you'll observe.

But, recovery footwork isn't the only thing you need to work on if you really want to improve your badminton footwork.

You also need to develop your internal clock.

What does this mean?

Well, whenever you play badminton, there's a particular pace that you're most comfortable with.

And when you're forced to play either above or below this pace, you're likely to make a lot of errors.

The good news is that you can train your internal clock so you're better able to play at different speeds.

There are four processes involved in training for pace in badminton.

The first is training your eyes.

After all, if you don't see the shuttle fast enough, then you'll most likely be late in your movement.

The second is training your reflexes, which helps you make a quick start from wherever you are on the court.

The third is conditioning your muscles so they perform faster.

And the fourth is testing new racket tensions once your skill has improved. Increased string tension allows the shuttle to leave your racket face much faster.

Now you know exactly what to train, but then, how do you do it?

Eye Training

The first thing you need to do is have your eyes tested to make sure you still have good eyesight.

You may then make full use of your good eyesight with a few exercises.

One good exercise involves covering the net with a non-see-through cloth and then asking someone to throw shuttles over the net for you to hit.

This helps enhance your ability to respond quickly with net shots.

Ask your exercise partner to vary the speed and direction of his feed so you'll really be trained to scan for the shuttle.

Reflex Training

Stand near midcourt, facing backwards.

Your exercise partner stands on the other side of the court and then shouts a command before throwing the shuttle your way.

You turn and hit the shuttle upon hearing the command.

This is a very useful exercise which you should keep developing over time.

You may increase the degree of difficulty by asking your partner to vary the target areas and speed of his throws.

Muscle Conditioning

When you work out, be sure to add exercises that train your muscles for power, not necessarily for adding bulk.

You'd also do well to play to music or skip to music.

Finally, you can perform half-court and full-court exercises as well to develop the speed of your muscles' reaction.

As long as you do these exercises regularly, you'll surely see significant improvements in your footwork very soon.

What's even better is that your overall badminton game will improve as well.

Take note that being able to play faster gives you a tactical advantage over your opponent, which is why it's very important to improve the speed at which you're able to spot the shuttle, your reaction time in moving towards the shuttle, and your recovery to base.

PART 8
How to Out-Manoeuvre, Outplay and Outscore Your Opponent

Have you ever walked off a badminton court wondering how you could have lost to someone whom you know is a much less-skilled player than you are?

Have you ever felt the frustration of getting so close to a win, yet never being able to make the necessary breakthrough?

If you've answered YES to these questions, then perhaps your problem isn't so much the lack of badminton skills, but the lack of an ability to read your opponent.

Regardless of whether you're a beginner or a professional, you'll definitely need to be able to identify your opponent's weaknesses and use them to your advantage.

Needless to say, you're going to play against badminton players with different styles of play.

These players will also have their own favourite shots, likes, and dislikes. And they will naturally have their own weaknesses as well.

Your goal should be to simplify your style of play and be able to assess your opponent's style as well.

Once you're able to achieve this, it'll be a lot easier for you to strategize and beat your opponent.

Here are the various styles of play and some easy ways to identify them:

1. Aggressive Attacking

This type of player is very easy to identify, as he is likely to try to attack in every single move.

These players usually prefer fast-paced games and are likely to favour the smash, in hopes of quickly finishing off the rally.

Take note that this player is ready to pounce on every single loose shot, so you'll have to make your shots carefully.

But, above everything else, what you must guard against is getting intimidated by this type of player.

2. Attacking Thinker

This type of player can be quite difficult to beat because they attack very well and are able to place their shots perfectly to achieve their desired results.

They like to mix up their pacing and they have more finesse than an attacker.

When playing against this type of player, you'll have to be constantly on your guard, especially around the net.

They may lack the aggression of the attacker, but they'll still bury a poor serve whenever they get the chance.

3. Aggressive Defender

This might come as a surprise, but there are players who prefer to counter-hit.

They're fond of setting up specific situations such that they can inject their own pace into the return shot, thus making it difficult for you to make a decent return.

These players like to move the shuttle around in order to expose your weaknesses.

Take note that these players have very good deception skills and are likely to send you the wrong way.

4. Defending Thinker

This type of player is very good at moving the shuttle around the court in a defensive way.

They favour lifting the shuttle and manoeuvring it to expose gaps in your attack.

They are also fond of deception and prefer a slower pace, which means there's less pressure when playing against this type of player.

They usually use lifting, blocking, and pushing returns to create openings.

5. The Complete Player

This type of player is a bit of a chameleon, as he can use all four styles of play.

The good news for you is that these players still have a favourite style among the four.

Your goal, therefore, is to identify which style they're more comfortable with.

You'll then have the option of learning to play well against that style or force your opponent to use the style he's least comfortable with.

PART 9
How to Execute a Killer Cross Drop

Many badminton enthusiasts out there have unfortunately not had the opportunity to learn how to execute a killer cross drop.

Well, you would have to, because this is one of the most valuable badminton skills you need to learn and master.

Knowing how to deliver a good cross drop can sometimes spell the difference between winning and losing a game.

The good news for you is that this article will tell you exactly how you can develop your skills at executing a badminton cross drop.

To be able to execute this badminton stroke successfully, you will, of course, need to first learn the badminton basics.

After all, you can't proceed to the more complex skills like the badminton cross drop unless you've built a strong foundation for your game.

And there are also several factors you need to take into consideration if you want to master the badminton cross drop.

Here are a few tips on how you can execute a killer cross drop successfully:

1. When you hold the badminton racket, be sure to do so in such a way that the racket face is positioned vertically and that it is in line with your hand.

   You should also make sure that the racket face is always open a little bit, so as to provide enough contact point for the shuttlecock.

2. Locate the exact point on your opponent's side of the court where you want the shuttle to land and

then aim for that specific spot when you strike.

And as you complete your shot, always be sure to follow through by turning your body forward.

At the same time, you should also step forward in order to complete the shot.

3. To make sure that your cross drop badminton strokes are executed correctly, your ending position should be such that the leg that's positioned in front is the same as the hand you use to hold the racket.

   This means that if hold the racket in your right hand, then your right leg should be in front when the shot is completed, and if you're a left-handed player, then your left leg should be in front as you complete the cross drop shot.

4. Now, all that's left for you to do is to keep practicing the steps outlined above in order for you to master the killer badminton cross drop shot.

   Just like any other stroke in any sport, it is through constant practice that you'll be able to master this shot and be so familiar with it that it becomes almost second nature to you.

   When you've achieved this, you'll be able to execute the cross drop effortlessly.

Well, now you know how to execute a killer cross drop in badminton.

All that's left is for you to decide if you're going to use this knowledge to your advantage or not.

In the same way, it's your responsibility to decide whether you want to improve your badminton game or simply enjoy the game itself without really trying too hard to become a better badminton player.

PART 10
How to Take Shots from Your Opponent

Badminton is a sport that many people love.

It's a good way to bond with family and friends, and it's a good form of exercise as well.

Of course, if you're playing badminton for competitive purposes, then you'll have to master the basic badminton skills and some more advanced techniques in order to become a good player and ensure a win in all of your games.

What only a few people know, however, is that becoming a good badminton player also requires learning how to take shots from your opponent.

In fact, this is one of the key strategies that'll ensure a win in a game of badminton.

And in order to successfully take a shot from your opponent, you'll have to prepare yourself carefully and be on constant alert for any and all shots.

This allows you to optimize every opportunity to turn your opponent's shots in your favour.

Being prepared means you need to place all of your focus on how your opponent hits the shuttle.

This includes watching how the shuttle leaves the racket face of your opponent.

And each time your opponent hits the shuttle, you should expect it to cross the net into your side of the court.

Take note as well that your opponent is likely to hit the shuttle away from you, so you should be alert and prepared at all times to hit the shuttle on the run.

One very effective way of getting to the shuttle quickly is by taking a small bouncy step and then sliding into position to hit the shuttle.

Of course, you should always remember to recover quickly back to your midcourt as soon as you've hit the return shot.

Even as you make the recovery, you should already expect your opponent to make a clean return shot.

If, for some reason, you feel that you won't be able to get to the shuttle in time, then stay right where you are while waiting for your opponent's move.

It's much easier to get to the shuttle from a standstill position than from a moving position.

Watch your opponent's racket as he prepares to hit the shuttle.

Focus on the shuttle and be sure to wait until you know exactly in which direction the shuttle will travel before you make your move.

Avoid anticipating the shuttle's movement too soon.

Once you've determined the direction of your opponent's shot, pivot with your dominant foot and then take a skipping action or a step-close-step motion.

Remember to always keep your feet close to the floor and cross them over when you hit a backhand shot.

When you approach the net, remember that your dominant leg should lead and push off when you return to your midcourt position.

You should also remember to lean backward whenever you bring your non-dominant foot forward and position it near your dominant foot.

The resulting push-off with both feet allows you to easily change direction and propels you back to midcourt even faster.

If you keep the above tips in mind, take them to heart, and apply them in every badminton game you play, you'll soon see a marked improvement in your overall game.

So, the next time you step on a badminton court, remember that the game isn't all about your ability to deliver killer shots; it's about being able to successfully take shots from your opponent as well.

PART 11
Choosing the Right Racket

Badminton is a popular sport, and if you're interested in getting into it, then you'll naturally have to master a few basic techniques.

More than that, however, you'll also have to choose the right equipment for the game.

Among the most important pieces of equipment in badminton is, of course, the racket.

You'll have to choose one that suits your playing style best, so as to enhance the skills you've worked so hard to develop.

Take note that buying a badminton racket can be quite daunting, since there are so many varieties currently available in the market, and each variety has its own advantages and disadvantages.

Some players decide to choose a racket based on brand name, but remember that popular brands are also more expensive.

And although these rackets are of top quality, that doesn't necessarily mean they're well-suited to your playing style.

Therefore, the decision as to which racket you should buy has to be based largely on your style of play.

Remember that no two players are the same and that every single player has his own set of strengths and weaknesses.

It's a good idea to be confident about your playing style first before you shell out a considerable amount on a high-end racket.

A good way to determine what type of racket fits your particular playing style is to seek the advice of your coach or of a professional badminton player.

Remember that the badminton racket you buy is the final piece of the puzzle that will complete your personality as a badminton player.

And unless all of the other pieces fall perfectly into place, your badminton racket will merely be an accessory and will not affect your skill in the sport at all.

Therefore, you'll have to postpone shopping for a top-quality racket until you've mastered all the basics, such as the different strokes and footwork.

Aside from the basic badminton skills and techniques, you also need to work on your fitness and physical strength.

It is therefore a good idea to hit the gym regularly in order to build muscles that'll lend more power to your shots.

Remember that no matter how many badminton rackets you try and regardless of how expensive your racket is, it won't do you any good unless you've taken care of all the basic requirements.

The strength of your wrist and your overall body strength are also among the most important considerations when choosing a badminton racket.

You should stay away from heavy rackets unless you have a very strong wrist.

Lighter rackets usually require more power in your hits, but they're also more suited to those who have less wrist strength.

Grip size should also be considered when shopping for a badminton racket.

You should choose a racket with a handle that's comfortable for you to grip.

If you can't grip the racket right, then you can't hit the shot right.

Of course, there's no guarantee that the right badminton racket for your playing style will come cheap.

But, still it's best to develop your skills first before buying an expensive racket to make sure the money you spend isn't wasted.

Be patient, work on improving your game, and it will surely be easier for you to choose the right badminton racket that'll help you bring your game to the next level.

PART 12
How to Prevent Injury in Badminton

There are several possible types of injuries you can potentially get as a result of playing badminton, and the most common of these are a sprained ankle, lower back pain, ligament tears, and tennis elbow.

If you plan to play the game for competition purposes, then you should take the necessary precautions to prevent these injuries.

Here are some of the things you can do:

1. Warm-up/Cool Down

The reason why professional players spend 30 minutes warming up before a game and another 30 minutes cooling down afterwards is because they know the dangers of skipping these sessions.

Failure to warm-up or cool down can result in muscle pulls, and not only does warm-up stretches help prevent muscle pulls, but they also give a boost to your performance during the game itself.

Therefore, you should refrain from being too eager to play when you get to the badminton court.

Always take the time to loosen up your muscles and make them more flexible as you prepare for your game.

2. Use the Right Technique

Take note that performing the wrong techniques in badminton does not only make you perform poorly, but may also lead to injuries.

For example, you should never take your non-racket arm for granted in a game of badminton.

Rather, you should use it to maintain balance as you play.

If you perform a smash without using your arm for balance, there's a big chance that you'll injure the muscles around your waist, thus causing lower back pain.

3. Choose the Right Racket

Choosing the wrong racket is also a common cause for injury in badminton.

Therefore, you should make sure the racket you buy is the one that's best suited to your playing style.

Seek advice from your coach or from a professional badminton player to know what type of racket will work best for you.

4. Choose the Right String Tension

Just as you have to choose the right badminton racket, you also need to use the right string tension in your racket.

Take note that higher tension are for control whereas lower tensions are for power.

Many professional badminton players use string tensions over 30lbs.

It would be a good idea for you to use tensions between 20 and 26lbs.

Remember that the higher the tension is, the less power you'll have in your strokes.

Take care not to try putting too much power into your strokes in order to prevent injury.

5. Use the Right Shoes

Badminton shoes are especially designed to absorb shocks and hard impacts.

Take note that the manner in which a badminton game is played can be harmful to your knee cap, which is why it's very important to use shoes that have good shock absorbers.

This helps prevent injuries to your knee caps and your shin bones.

6. Avoid Playing for Too Long

You should know by now that too much of anything is bad for you.

This is true of badminton as well.

Playing for too long is likely to hurt your shin bones, knee caps, or ankles, since the game requires you to constantly lunge forward to receive the shuttle.

As with anything else, injury can be prevented if you play the game in moderation.

NOTES

Printed in Great Britain
by Amazon